RIPKEN

CAL ON CAL

Text by Cal Ripken
Photographs by Walter Iooss, Jr.
Edited by Mark Vancil

THE SUMMIT PUBLISHING GROUP
One Arlington Centre, 1112 East Copeland Road, Fifth Floor
Arlington, Texas 76011

Printed in the United States of America

99 98 97 96 95   5 4 3 2

Library of Congress Cataloging-In-Publication Data

Ripken, Cal 1960-
    Ripken: Cal on Cal / photographs by Walter Iooss, Jr. ; edited
by Mark Vancil.
        p. cm.
    ISBN 1-56530-194-3 (hardcover)
    1. Ripken, Cal, 1960-   . 2. Baseball players—United States—
Biography. 3. Baseball players—United States—Pictorial works. 4.
Baltimore Orioles (Baseball team) I. Iooss, Walter. II. Vancil, Mark,
1958-   . III. Title.
GV865.R47A3 1995b
796.357'092—dc20
[B]   96-41508
                                                          CIP

SPECIAL THANKS:
    Laura Sadovi-Vancil
at the Tufton Group:
    Ira Rainess
    Desiree Pilachowski
at The Baltimore Orioles:
    John Maroon
    Bill Stetka

Design by
David Sims

Color separation by
Network Graphics, Fort Worth, Texas

Printed by
Berryville Graphics
a Bertelsmann company

I R O N

*"Early in my career,
I decided I never wanted to
get out of shape."*

10

M A N

*"Compared to how my dad
has lived his life, I'm not
even close."*

46

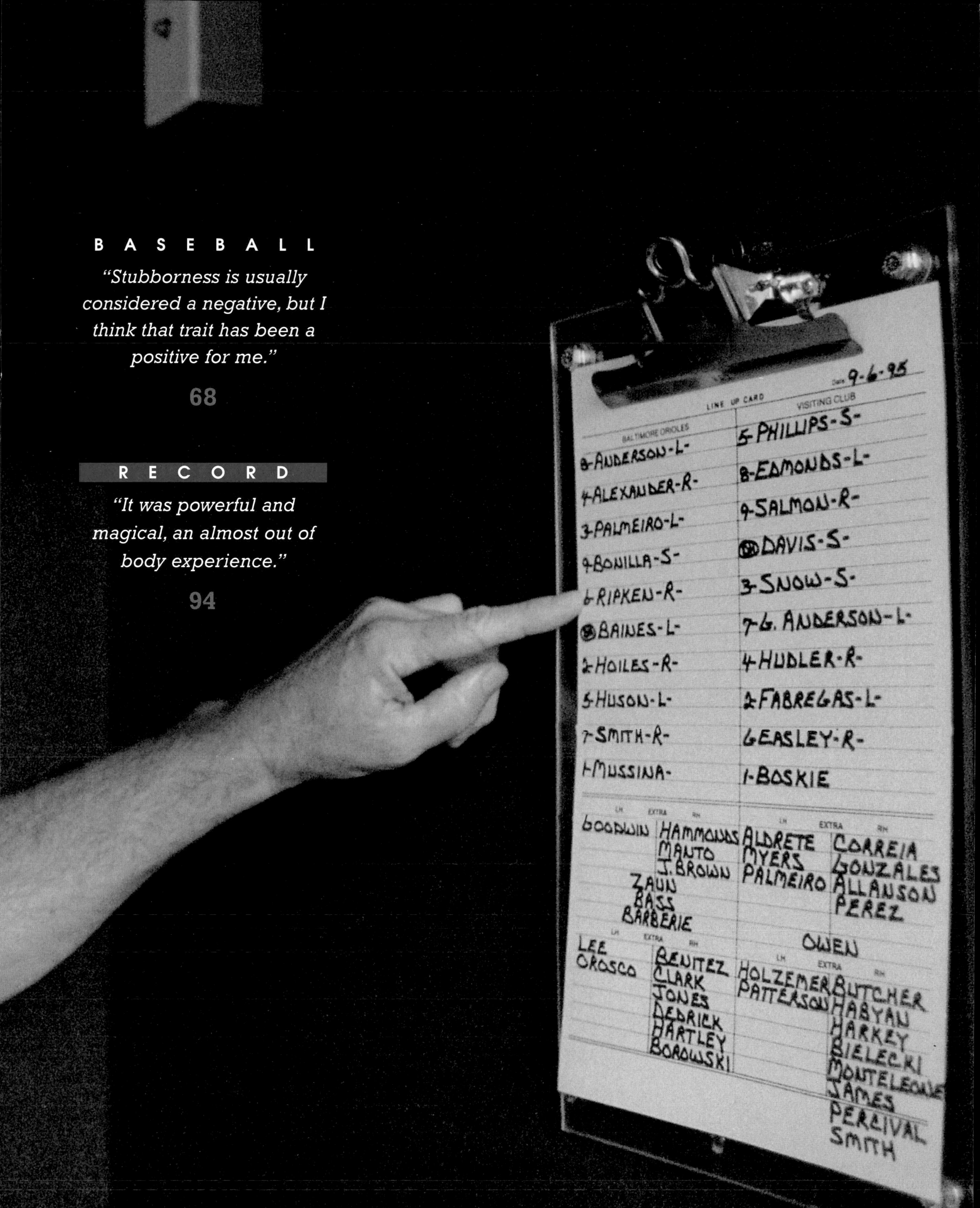
9-6-95
LINE UP CARD
BALTIMORE ORIOLES
VISITING CLUB
8-ANDERSON-L-
4-ALEXANDER-R-
3-PALMEIRO-L-
9-BONILLA-S-
6-RIPKEN-R-
BAINES-L-
2-HOILES-R-
5-HUSON-L-
7-SMITH-R-
1-MUSSINA-
5-PHILLIPS-S-
8-EDMONDS-L-
9-SALMON-R-
DAVIS-S-
3-SNOW-S-
7-G. ANDERSON-L-
4-HUDLER-R-
2-FABREGAS-L-
6-EASLEY-R-
1-BOSKIE
GOODWIN
HAMMONDS
MANTO
J. BROWN
ZAUN
BASS
BARBERIE
ALDRETE
MYERS
PALMEIRO
CORREIA
GONZALES
ALLANSON
PEREZ
OWEN
LEE
OROSCO
BENITEZ
CLARK
JONES
DEDRICK
HARTLEY
BOROWSKI
HOLZEMER
PATTERSON
BUTCHER
HABYAN
HARKEY
BIELECKI
MONTELEONE
JAMES
PERCIVAL
SMITH

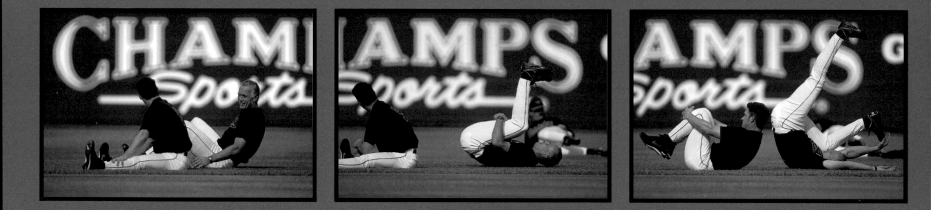

"Early in my career, I decided I never wanted to get out of shape."

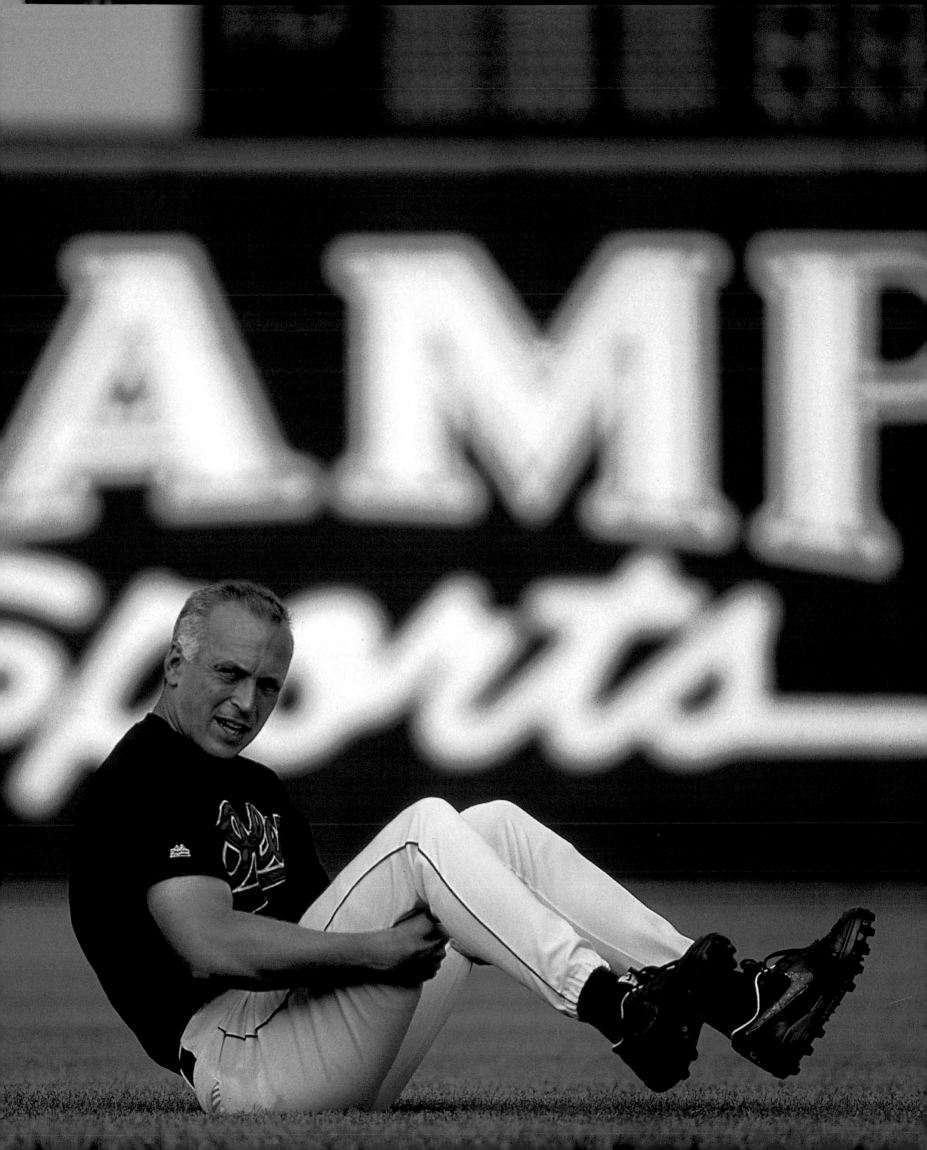

EARLY IN MY CAREER, I decided I never wanted to get out of shape. I thought the process of getting back into shape in time for spring training would increase the risk of getting injured. It seemed pretty simple to me: Take care of yourself and reduce the chance of injury. That thought became my guide.

Although I never really had a structured workout schedule when I was younger, I stayed active. There might be a racquetball game during the day and then a pick-up basketball game at night. I just did whatever I could.

Now I take roughly three weeks off to make the transition from playing to getting into my off-season routine. If we don't get into the World Series, then my off-season starts Nov. 1. I'll lift weights for three or four weeks, three times a week for 90 minutes a day just to get my body familiar with the program. After the initial phase, I go into a strength-building phase which takes me into the middle of January. I really don't get too carried away with trying to make huge weight-lifting gains, but I am doing six days a week on my upper and lower body.

I also make sure I'm doing skill level workouts at the same time so I don't throw off my timing and balance. I need to make sure my muscles fire when I need them. So I hit in the cage at home three days a week, slowly increasing the time. I have a routine where I hit off a tee to get loose and then work an additional 15 to 20 minutes off the machine. So my actual hitting time would be 35 to 40 minutes three times a week.

I also throw on my skill days, which might be Tuesday, Thursday, and Saturday. Monday, Wednesday, Friday, and sometimes on Saturday and Sunday I play basketball. When you add it all up, I'm working six days a week and I'm hitting a little bit of everything.

I've always thought every athlete has only a small window of opportunity to play any sport. Take care of yourself and you maximize that window. I've applied that philosophy to my workouts.

THE GYM IS SOMETHING I thought about since I was a kid. I always told myself that if I ever got in the position, I was going to build my own gym. But those thoughts were motivated by my desire to play basketball, not baseball. I remember watching NBA games on Sunday afternoons. At halftime I'd always get the itch to play. It might be the middle of winter, but I'd go outside for as long as I could take the cold. I'd dribble, shoot, and try to practice what I had just seen on the television.

There wasn't a gym, not even a health club or a YMCA around where you could play basketball. So I figured, "I'm going to grow up and be a baseball player. And I'll build myself a gym one day." My mom always tried to help us keep our dreams in perspective. I remember her saying, "Well, you could make some money and buy a farm. And on that farm there might be a big barn you could gut out and turn into a gym."

I was terrible at drawing things, but I remember spending a lot of time drawing that farm and what the barn would look like with my gym inside.

So when I got to the big leagues, I spent almost two years looking at farms. And they had to have a barn. I would have been content building a gym and putting in a bedroom instead of building a complete house. I just needed a place to stay and play. I really would have been content with that.

But my representatives talked me into building the house first, thinking that this young 24-year-old doesn't know what he's talking about. I'm sure they thought that this thing about the gym would pass. Eventually I went ahead anyway. It was easy to rationalize, even to my representatives, because I put in a batting cage and a weight room. But I really wanted it for the basketball court.

I'VE SEEN PLAYERS at the end of their careers experiencing the deterioration of their physical ability. If you ask any athlete what happens at the end, you'll hear consistently, "Your legs are the first to go."

It makes sense. Once you lose your legs, especially when you play a position like shortstop, everything else isn't far behind. So early on, I developed a theory to delay that process as long as possible. In order to maintain younger legs, I was going to push harder and do different activities, maybe even stressful activities, to keep my legs working.

With basketball, the risks are obvious. I could get injured because I'm putting extra stress on my legs, tendons, and joints, stress not necessarily of the kind that comes from playing baseball. But I also know the benefits have translated directly onto the baseball field. I think basketball has extended the life of my legs because I've continued to push myself instead of thinking, "I'm too old to be doing this or that."

By pushing harder, the explosiveness gained by incorporating the game into my workouts has helped my legs stay young. For me, that means staying at shortstop instead of being forced over to third base because I can't move any longer.

THE KID INSIDE ME says, "You only want this place so the kids can have a big playroom and you can play along with them." That's just who I am as a person.

On the intellectual or analytical side, I know my job goes 12 months a year, so I need somewhere I can go to get myself prepared to work.

But I had all kinds of other plans when I started building the gym. I put in a rubber floor so I could play street hockey, take ground balls, and play tennis. We have great hockey games in there. None of us can skate, but that's not the purpose of those games. We run, sweat, get a great workout, and it's fun. We have guys come over and hit in the cage, and the gym has become an extension of the fun I have during a normal baseball season.

I GENERALLY WORK OUT alone, so I'm forced to be self-motivated. I started running up a hill near the side of my house a few years ago right around the time people first started writing and talking about maybe moving me to third base the next season.

The hill is a half mile straight up. I'd tell myself if I didn't run the hill, then no matter what else I did, I'd wind up playing third base within a year. I'd think about third base every time I started up that hill.

THERE WERE TWO bits of advice I received from my dad and mom when I went off to the minor leagues, and both of them concerned eating.

My dad told me not to be afraid to spend my money. In other words, the meal money (which was around six dollars a day) wasn't going to cover my meals. He told me that food is the fuel for my body and that I wouldn't be able to go out and play every day or physically do what's necessary if I didn't eat right.

My mom told me to learn how to cook. She always gave me recipes and advice about the basic food groups. And I've always worked off that idea of eating vegetables and salads.

I am regimented in the sense that if I have a night game, I make sure I eat twice before I get to the ballpark. Sometimes I wake up, eat, and go back to sleep. If we arrive in a city at three or four in the morning, I'll set the alarm for 10:50 A.M. so I can order breakfast before the kitchen switches to lunch.

I'll order, go back to sleep until the food arrives, get up, eat, and go back to sleep again, knowing I'll have time to eat once more before I leave for the ballpark.

For me, my entire approach to nutrition is born out of those two bits of advice I received from my parents.

SOME OF THE best moments I've had in baseball haven't necessarily been on the field. You can derive a lot of satisfaction from getting big hits or making plays in critical situations, but a lot of the best times are in the preparation, the joking in the clubhouse, and the people you meet along the way.

There was a kid in Boston who used to be the visiting clubhouse boy. When we went in there last season, I ended up talking to him after the game. He went from the clubhouse to working security, and now he's a teacher getting a master's degree. You remember guys like that, joking around with them and all the fun you've had. And you spend so many more hours inside the clubhouse either preparing for the game or relaxing after it's over. So I'm building a real locker room connected to my gym. It's going to be my place, the kind of place I've lived in my whole life, a place that holds special memories.

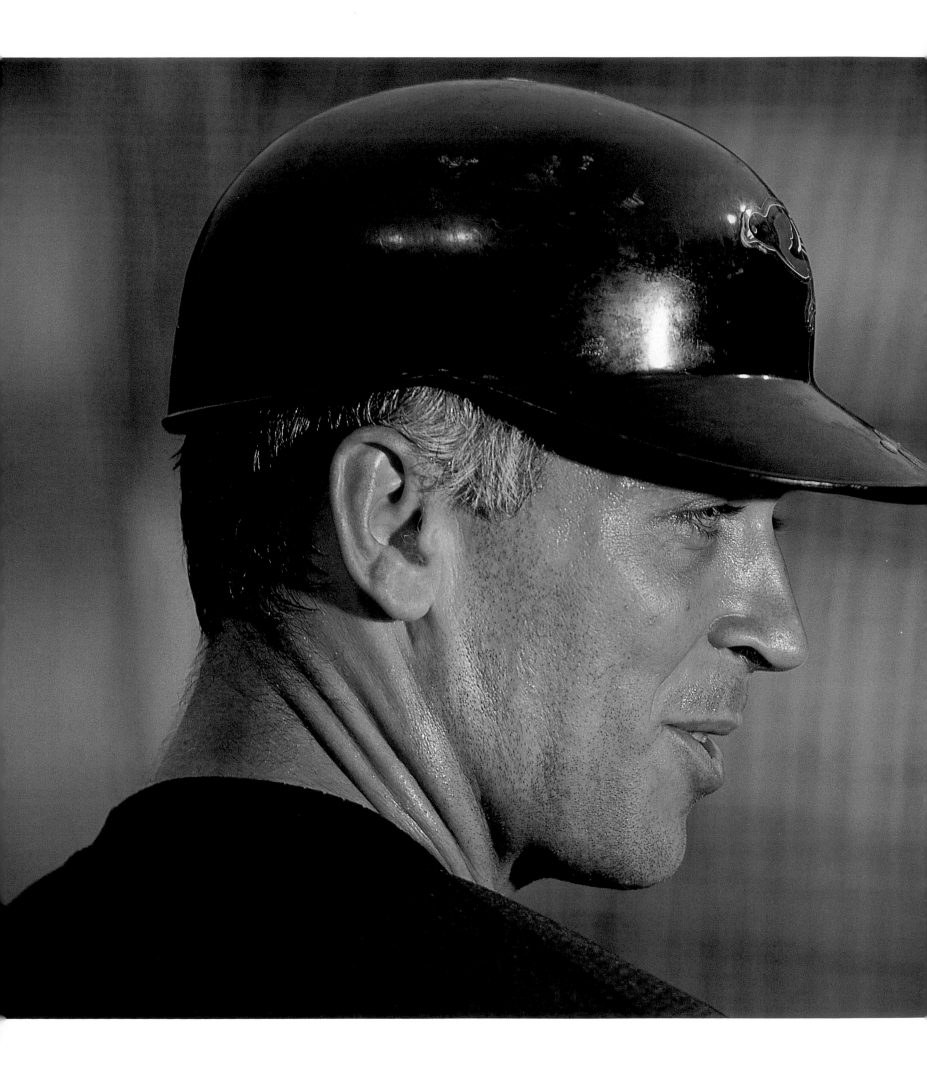

COMPETITION IS SOMETHING all athletes need. I like to get a dose of it every day if possible. In the off-season, I usually get mine through basketball. But I need a contest, something to test my competitive edge, my desire to win.

We went to a place in Arizona before spring training. There were all kinds of activities, hikes through canyons, things I'd never done. It was fun, but the activities lacked that competitiveness. You were only competing against yourself, trying to see if you could climb up a mountain. But no one was racing or being timed to see who won.

So I found myself looking for that competition, that challenge. I'm not a racquetball player, but I'm coordinated enough to hit the ball off the wall, and I understand angles. I also love the competition and the workout from playing. So I ended up paying the instructor to beat the crap out of me. I told him I understood that the better the players are, the less the workout, because they know where to place the ball.

I said, "I'm not interested in seeing whether you can kill the shot. I want you to work me out, and I want you to hit the ball so the points are long and you run me around the court." And he did. But I derived a good feeling from getting the crap beaten out of me because there was a challenge and a sense of accomplishment when I'd get a point.

I look for that kind of competition in a workout because you can't create them on your own. You need other people to help you do that.

MY DAD HAD a certain way of bringing importance to every game, whether he was playing, coaching, or managing. When he played, catchers didn't have the kinds of gloves they have now. So they were taught to catch with two hands.

But foul tips often would hit that bare right hand. Sometimes the impact would knock off a fingernail or tear back the skin to the point bone was exposed.

He would tell us all these gory things, and we'd say, "Well, what did you do?" I remember one time he said Earl Weaver came out and saw my dad's finger torn back with blood all over the place. Earl said, "Come on, we're taking you out of the game." And my dad called him a name and said, "You're not taking me out of this game. I'm staying." Earl said, "What do you mean? You've got a bone sticking out of your hand. How are you going to play?" My dad said, "Well, I'll just tape these two fingers together and get back to playing." That was my dad's mentality. The trainer threw a little tape on his fingers, and he stayed in the game. But the best example of his toughness was when he played soccer. He might get

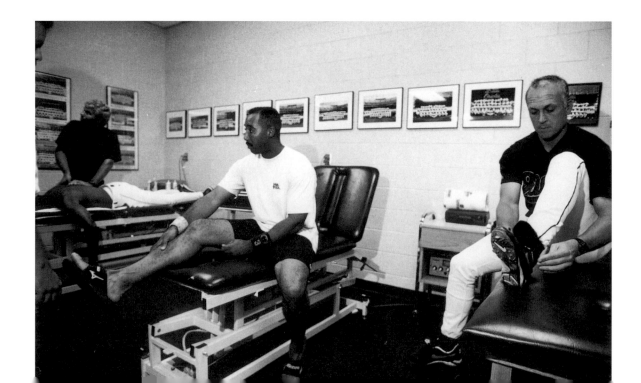

stepped on, kick the ground, or kick the ball a certain way and blood would form under the toenail. The pressure could cause a lot of pain. When my dad got home, he would pull out his power drill, put in a bit, and drill into the nail. Blood would squirt out, and he'd just put some tape on it, and that was that.

He downplayed injuries even when we were kids. If you fell off your bike or skinned your knee, he'd check to see if you were all right and say things like, "It'll be all right before you're married twice," or "You'll be all right once it stops hurting," or "Rub a little tobacco juice on it, and it'll be all right."

I remember thinking, "Where are we going to get some tobacco juice?" He just treated most things like they were nothing. So I grew up playing through minor injuries. If I foul a ball off my leg, yeah, it hurts, but I can play. My attitude toward injuries was drilled into me when I was young.

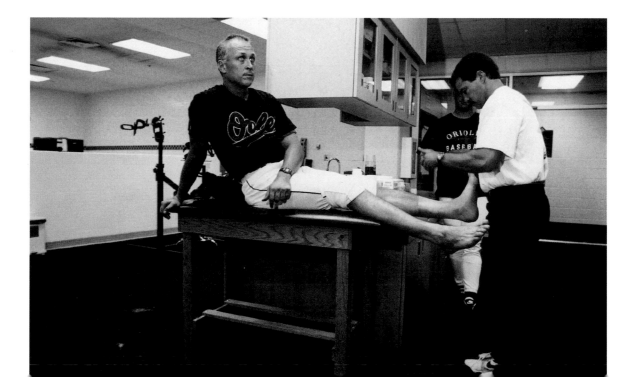

WHEN I WAS PLAYING sandlot ball, or even in the minor leagues, I always felt like I knew more than my coaches. It really didn't seem strange to me because I just had a different set of circumstances growing up. And a lot of times the coach would use me as a resource.

He would ask, "How does your dad do this?" or "How does he take infield or batting practice?" I was always asked to contribute to the way practice was run, or to provide some sense of order.

Even when I went to the minor leagues, I knew that some of the things I was being told were wrong. Instinctively, I didn't think they were the Oriole way. Sometimes I'd get on the phone and tell my dad. But my dad would say, "You have to listen to what they say because they are in charge. Try it their way but remember what's right. Always remember there is something you can gain from everyone. Maybe nine out of ten things are wrong, but try to extract that one idea that can help your game."

And that's how I've always tried to approach baseball. I remember giving that same advice to my brother, Billy. He'd call me and say, "They're telling me to do cutoffs and relays this way, and I know it's wrong." I ended up telling him the same thing: Try it, but remember how it's supposed to be done.

I'VE TRIED A LOT of different things to maintain my physical condition. Brady Anderson has brought me some ideas from track which he uses in his training. I've introduced some plyometrics, but only on a small level.

I've had to come a long way from the old school philosophy of training. When I was younger, my dad and people from his generation believed weights and baseball didn't mix. Others said I shouldn't play basketball because I'd be using different muscles and risk injury. I've developed my own opinions, and I have never taken any advice at face value.

I'm very cautious and very skeptical. I had to learn to believe in weight training before I could ever get into it. I couldn't simply rely on someone's word or belief. Even though the strength coach has been brought into baseball, and conditioning has become so much more specific, I have to actually try it and see how my body reacts before adopting anything new.

I ask a lot of questions. I talked to Carlton Fisk after he went on a weight program and hit all those home runs one year. I ask a lot of questions. Anybody I meet, especially guys in different sports, I ask them what they are doing.

I DON'T KNOW if I could put my approach into words; but if I did, I'm sure it would sound like my dad's, something like "Nothing's worth doing halfway." I heard my dad say those words, and I witnessed him living his life by them. I do know that with baseball, if you're going to practice hitting or taking ground balls, you can't mess around. There is a right way to go about doing everything, even something as minor as picking up balls around the batting cage. Picking up balls is a good example because it was one of my dad's pet peeves. Between hitting groups, which are usually divided into 15 minute sessions for each four- or five-man group, the clock starts ticking on the next group as soon as the first one finishes. If you start at five o'clock, then the next group starts at exactly 5:15.

But you have to pick up balls around the cage before the first hitter steps in. You pick 'em up and run 'em out to the mound for the new batting practice pitcher. We call it "cleaning the carpet." But some guys drag their bat behind them, grab one ball at a time, and casually walk out to the mound.

My dad would always say, "Put your bat down, run in there, pick up balls, and get off the damn field." Picking up balls is no big thing, but there is a practical, functional way of doing it correctly.

Most players probably don't understand that minutes are ticking away, and you're taking time away from your group. You have an obligation to them to get in there and get the balls off the field. It's the difference between the right way to do things and the wrong way. If you're going to do it, you might as well do it correctly.

ANYTHING GOES until about a half hour before the game. Some people call it "putting on your game face." I don't necessarily think I have a game face, but my routine kicks in, and I start to mentally prepare for the game. The atmosphere becomes more serious—not as relaxed. I guess my demeanor changes a little bit. That might be particularly important in baseball because we play every day.

Still, when you play the game over and over again, your mind can drift.

One night Manny Alexander was at second base. I knew the situation, so I told him, "You've got the pickoff with a left-hander on the mound. You have responsibility for the double play, coverage on the steal, and coverage on a pickoff at first base if the guy runs."

So there's one out, and I relaxed. Then a ground ball went to third, and Jeff Huson threw to second to start a double play. For a split second, I didn't know how many outs there were. There was this little drift. All of a sudden, I was expecting Jeff to throw the ball to second for a force and we'd run off the field.

Then Manny turned the double play, and I thought, "Oh yeah, one out." Other times it's just so easy because no matter what unfolds, you are so into the game—so sharp that you don't even have to remind yourself of the situation. Your concentration is right there.

"Compared to how my dad has lived his life, I'm not even close."

COMPARED TO HOW my dad has lived his life, I'm not even close. When I'm not playing baseball, I can hang my clothes on a chair and leave my shoes around. When I had my townhouse I could forget to take the trash out on trash day, and it didn't bother me one bit. If we missed a trash day at home, all hell would break loose. It didn't matter that the trash bin was only half full, and you could wait to the next trash day. It was the fact that we had to take out the trash on the day it was supposed to be done.

On rainy days when there was nothing to do, we would sort nuts and bolts. He'd have us match them up by sizes, organize them, and put them in jars or coffee cans. My dad was

the kind of person who, if you were discarding a lawn mower he'd say, "Are you throwing that out? Do you mind if I take it?" He would fix it or, if it wasn't fixable, use the spare parts.

My dad's garage is as meticulous as he is. It's not like he has beautiful custom cabinets. He retrofits an old dresser or something else to make the cabinets he has. I look at that garage and think, "Man, it's got to take a long time to do that."

So I guess it's not surprising that my approach to baseball comes from being around my father.

Ｍｙ DAUGHTER IS five and one-half, and we relate well to one another. We play all kinds of games, but she's totally different than my son. You have to play with her things because she's all girl.

Sometimes I think I relate better to her because my son is nonstop. He'll just wear you out because he wants to do the same thing over and over again, which I'm sure has always been a part of my personality, too. It's all physical with him. But it's challenging when your daughter asks you a "why" question. She's just soaking everything up.

WHEN I WAS YOUNGER, all my energies were channeled into becoming a ballplayer. Once I became a professional player in the minor leagues, everything revolved around my baseball schedule. Even when I reached the big leagues, it was more of the same because I was trying to establish myself and my career.

But the whole process impacts the balance you need in life. There was an emptiness that baseball didn't completely fill. I derived satisfaction from the success I had, but as a person there was a certain loneliness.

Eddie Murray and I probably hooked up because we had a lot in common. We were among the few single guys on the team.

We were playing and doing well, but I remember a couple times coming back from a Sunday afternoon game on the road. It would be seven or eight o'clock at night, and all the families would be at the airport picking up the players. Kids would be running up and hugging them. Eddie and I would be standing there waiting for the bus to the satellite parking lot. Although we never really talked about it, I think he kind of felt the same emptiness I did.

For all the great things that were happening, I didn't have anyone to share them with, no one there solely for me.

But like a lot of events in my life when there has been a need or a desire, everything seems to come together at the right time. And that's what happened with Kelly.

Al Bumbry and I were standing in a restaurant during the winter after our World Series title in 1983, and Kelly's mother recognized me. She was having dinner with her husband, Bob, and came over and asked for an autograph. She said, "My daughter doesn't really like baseball all that much, but she likes you." She kind of gave me the standard line, which I had heard a lot being single, something like, "Have I got a daughter for you."

So, not being very creative, I didn't know what to write. But something hit me at that moment, and I wrote, "To Kelly, if you look anything like your mother, I'm sorry I missed you." And I signed my name.

Three weeks later I was out, and Kelly was with a friend. She came up to me and thanked me for being nice to her mom. She was very pretty, and I was immediately attracted to her. When she said that about her mom I quickly replayed the situation in my mind. I'm very bad with names, but I remembered hers.

I said, "Wait a minute. You're Kelly." I guess I took that as a sign, and we started dating. It was strange, one of those fateful things, I guess. I still don't know why I was able to recall her name. I can remember what Jim Rice did in a game in 1983, if you give me enough information about the game. I can probably tell you the pitch sequence and everything else. But when it comes to other things, my memory isn't quite so good. So for me to remember her name…

But what attracted me to Kelly was that she is strong and independent. In that sense, she's like my mother. I lived with my dad being absent a lot. My mom was there all the time, and she was the one responsible for all us kids. When we had to pack up and drive across country, my mom was in charge. If we broke down in a small town, my mom took care of us and made the decisions.

WHEN YOU HAVE kids and see what they pick up and how they do things, you examine yourself. You realize they are just doing what you do, so I find myself examining why I do things a certain way. I realize I do them that way because that's how my father did them, that it's a direct reflection of how my parents did them.

I remember when it would snow a lot and we'd be out shoveling with my father. Some people would shovel only a narrow path. We had to shovel to the edge of the walk. So when the snow melted, the sidewalks would be really neat and perfect all the way around. My dad also used to go around and shovel the neighborhood when we were kids. I think that he was away so much that maybe he wanted them to look out for his family when he was out of town.

So when Billy and I started shoveling around the townhouse I lived in, you could tell we did it differently than everyone else because ours was perfect. And before you know it, we're shoveling out somebody else's sidewalk. We kind of looked at each other and laughed because we realized we were doing it just like Dad.

MY BOY IS so physically blessed. I'm sure most fathers think the same thing. But I see how Ryan picks things up quickly. My daughter, Rachel, isn't as much of a copycat as my son.

I did something interesting when Ryan was a small child. When he couldn't walk yet, I'd bring his little rocker into the gym, put him on the floor, and shoot baskets. He would just sit there and giggle.

He really hadn't shown any signs of being a person yet. That's how young he was. It was my way of being with him, and it was an easy way to keep him entertained. As soon as he got a little older and gained some coordination, he started shooting a basketball. Now he watches how I shoot and tries to do the same things, though he's a lefty.

I remember when he threw a ball that bounced off my head. I didn't even know he could throw. I wondered how he knew what to do, but part of my training is throwing balls into a cage. He had picked up on the mechanics. I mean, he lifts his leg up when he throws, and you can't teach that. He just does it.

I might be practicing dunking, and I'd hang on the rim. He loved that. Right away he started pointing to the rim. So I held him up to the basket, and he threw the ball down and hung there. I let his legs go, and he just hangs there laughing. And he's two years old! He's been hanging on things like that forever. My wife is six feet tall, and to this day she says I married her because I was trying to breed a basketball player. There might be some truth to that.

I KNOW I WANTED to copy everything my dad did—how he dressed, how he put on his baseball uniform. I thought my dad knew the right way to do everything.

I don't know why, but I see the same things in my daughter and my son. My daughter copies my wife. My son watches me. I didn't teach Ryan to take a little car and drive it over my head making car sounds. Boys do boy things, and girls do other things. There are similarities, of course. The other day, my son was pushing around a baby carriage. He thought that was the most fun thing to do.

But he watches me so closely. The way he throws is something he's been doing since before he was two. I caught him watching me throw one day in the cage. I picked up the balls at one end and threw them to the other. I threw the same way every time, very precisely.

Out of the corner of my eye I caught him picking up balls, just like I was doing, winding up and throwing. It was almost like he had his own motion. Most kids just flick their wrist. Here's this little man picking his leg up and throwing.

The difference for me growing up was that there were four kids all vying for some special time with my dad. There were certain things I recognized early on that my other brothers and sister didn't want to do. One of them was getting up on Saturday mornings and going to baseball clinics with my dad. You'd have to get out of bed instead of sleeping in or watching cartoons.

He would come and ask all of us if we wanted to go. So after I heard the rest of them say no, I hopped up. I did it for selfish reasons, because I would have time alone with my dad. I cherished the time we had in the car together to and from those clinics.

I could ask him anything. It was just a special time. That's why I place so much importance on driving my daughter to school. I don't know whether she looks at it that way, but I do. I want to be there and participate as much as possible, and driving her to school is one of those special moments when we're out of the group family setting and just alone with one another.

Sometimes Rachel will sing songs, and other times she'll say, "Daddy, I want to tell you something." Maybe I'm forcing the issue a little bit, but I know how much that time with my dad meant to me.

"Stubbornness is usually considered a negative, but I think that trait has been a positive for me."

STUBBORNNESS IS USUALLY considered a negative, but I think that trait has been a positive for me. But I think of myself as being open-minded, too, and trying to see both sides of everything I do.

But one of the most unfair parts of the consecutive-games streak has been the comparisons between myself and Lou Gehrig. I understand why the connection is made, but we play different positions, and he's one of the best players ever to play baseball. I know I'm not.

I'm a good player. I've mapped out a good career, and I'm happy with what I've done with my talents. But it's unfair to make statistical comparisons between us. He was one of the greatest players of all time, and no one should forget that.

But if there is any comparison to be made, then maybe it's that we have a certain love for the game—a certain will and desire to play. Maybe we share a common approach—the idea that it's important to go out there and play every day because it's a team game. Maybe we share the same commitment to play day in and day out.

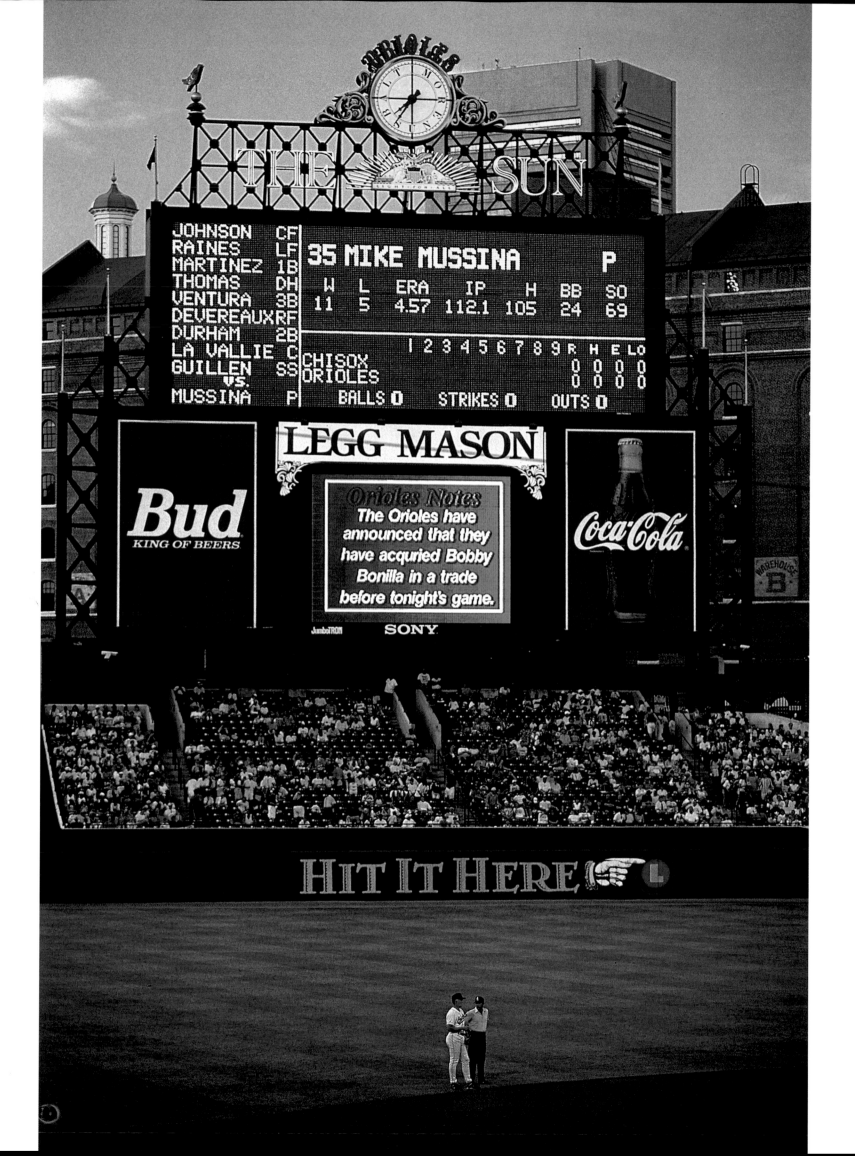

EVERY PLAYER HAS a responsibility to understand what his contribution to the team must be and what it means. If you're a hitter in the middle of the lineup, then you have to learn how to drive in runs.

If you're a hit-and-run guy, then you have to work on becoming better at moving the ball around and moving guys over. If you're required to bunt, then you have to practice bunting skills to keep them sharp, because that's what you do for the team.

In spring training when we have 15 minutes for bunting practice, you know some guys are just putting in the time. You know that in crunch time they're not going to be able to come through.

Other people take it seriously and say to themselves, "For the 15 minutes I'm here I'm going to bear down. I'm going to make sure I figure out what I need to do to get these bunts down."

That's the kind of approach I learned from my dad. That's what he expected every time, and that's what I expect of myself. Even in bunting practice, I try to figure out games or competitions. We have ten bunts? I can make ten better bunts than you. Or maybe we'll put obstacles down to make it more difficult. Whatever it takes.

IN BASEBALL, if you're having a bad day there aren't many adjustments a player can make. I can't move in a little closer or use the backboard to help me like I can on the basketball court.

In that sense, the game is unique. In basketball, a great player can contribute in other ways if he's not shooting well. Even football players can throw a block.

But when you're swinging badly in baseball, and you're playing every day, even the worst pitcher (who's at the major league level and still pretty good) can make you look terrible.

REMEMBER MARK BELANGER calling me over when I first came up in 1981. We were in Detroit. He told me I should get into the habit of watching other players work at my position. He said that I could learn from watching them, good or bad.

One guy he wanted me to watch was Alan Trammell. Belanger said, "You should watch that guy a lot because he does things really well. Ever since he came into the league he's shown he knows how to play." Tram really impressed Belanger.

To this day some of the strangest things that pop into my head are things Belanger told me. When I was seventeen and taking ground balls at the ballpark side-by-side with him, Belanger would talk to me about making plays. I had no clue how I would ever understand what he was talking about. At that stage in my development, he was so far advanced I couldn't conceive making a play the way he was telling me to.

For example, take a slow hit ball in the hole. You can get in front of the ball, but the runner—someone like Kenny Lofton—might be fast. So you cheat on the backhand by getting your body in position to throw before you catch the ball. If you get in front of the ball, then you have to plant and throw.

Fundamentally, you are taught to take the backhand off your left foot, and the reason is that you want to have maximum reach. If you're on your left leg, you can reach farther. When you make the play correctly, then you plant your right foot and make the throw.

By being in position to throw when you catch the ball, you eliminate one or two steps. When he was explaining this would be something to use against a speedy runner, I could not grasp the concept. I remember thinking, "that's just Mark Belanger."

Then, sure enough, one day it happened instinctively. And Belanger's words came echoing back. I was seventeen years old when he explained that play, and it might not have clicked in until I was twenty-seven.

NOTHING REALLY CHANGED when my father became my manager with the Orioles. It had been kind of weird when I first got to the majors. But I quickly understood that he was a coach and I was a player. Even though I recognized that he was my father and that I'd go out to dinner with him after games sometimes, baseballwise he had his function and I had mine. When he became manager, it was just an extension of those responsibilities.

In professional baseball there is no preferential treatment. It's not like Little League, where the coach's son gets special treatment.

It's a hardened game at the professional level. If you don't deserve to be there, then you're going to be weeded out long before your father could hope to save you. If you're not hitting or playing defense well, the statistics and evaluations are right out in the open. It doesn't matter who your father is because there's nothing he can do.

And there really wasn't anything I could do when he was fired. Who would it have served if I had become publicly upset? There was no real reason for it. Sure, I had frustration and anger, but I had to deal with it the best I could for all concerned. It didn't serve anyone to lash out.

When my dad was advising me at the time, he said, "Don't worry about me. You have your job and your responsibilities." He told me I was in control of myself, I wasn't in control of what everybody else did.

He was the one who was victimized, so if he could make a statement like that to me and put things into perspective, then it should have been pretty easy for me to move on.

Looking back, it was a rough time. It was hard, a challenge and a period of time I wish I didn't have to experience. But I think I was able to at least have a broader perspective and a better understanding.

I STILL GET BUTTERFLIES in big moments while standing in the on-deck circle. The drama constantly builds in baseball. As a player, you're cast into a situation where you can make a difference. Experience tells me I have to control the emotion, channel that anxiety into something constructive.

The greatest times are those moments when I'm able to channel emotion into total concentration. I mean *total concentration*. When I'm hitting well, it almost seems like everything has gone from regular speed to slow motion, and I can deal with whatever comes.

I STEP INTO THE BOX, and I don't know what the pitcher is going to throw, but I see the ball the moment it's released. Everything slows down and it gets quiet. The sensation is unbelievable. I wish I was able to reach that level of concentration every time, but I can't.

It's one of the eeriest feelings an athlete can experience. The fans are screaming, I'm nervous, uptight, focused on doing well. All of a sudden, everything locks in. I'm in complete control. The pitcher gets ready to throw, and the ball starts coming in slow motion.

I see it coming in and I make contact. The ball takes off. Everything remains in slow motion until the ball reaches the outfield or goes over the wall. Then everything returns to fast action. As I'm running the bases, the sound comes back. The next thing I know, I'm standing on second base with a double. I've just knocked in three runs, and I'm

standing there thinking, "God, that was great." It's almost like a movie sequence, a feeling and mood that somebody else creates around you.

But it doesn't happen all the time. When I'm in that zone, my concentration is so precise and my focus is right there. I'm not thinking about anything else—nothing is on my mind or lurking in my subconscious.

And it doesn't matter who's pitching or how nasty the pitches are. When I'm in that zone, the ball moves slowly. Everything feels effortless. I don't even feel like I'm swinging the bat very hard or reacting quickly.

I've seen myself when in that zone on a television replay, and my perception of what happened at that moment is completely different from what I'm seeing. It looks like I reached for the ball, got the bat on it, boom, boom, boom.

But when it was happening, it's like I saw the ball coming in and realized, "Oh, here comes a breaking ball." And as it's breaking, I'm thinking, "OK, well, I better reach out over the plate and hit it."

Most of the time I know that if I'm looking for a ninety-mile-an-hour fastball and the guy has a nasty forkball, I'm not able to hit one if I'm looking for the other.

But when I get into that zone, I can be looking for that ninety-mile-an-hour fastball, but right when he's about to release the pitch I recognize, "Oh, that's a forkball." I just see it and my body takes over and I hit it. "How did I do that?"

Years when everything kind of fell into place for me, like 1983 and 1991, I was in that zone a lot more than other years. It makes you wonder what causes that to happen. How do you get there more often? I think the more you try, the less apt you are to get there, because I really think it has something to do with your ability to relax and let your talent and abilities come together.

It can happen for a period of time. I can ride a hot streak, or a groove. It's incredible when it's happening, which is why there are so many people out there trying to figure out how you can get there on demand. How do you hone your concentration to the point that you go into that zone regularly?

I don't believe anyone has the answer. But when it happens, it's the greatest feeling in sports.

I wish I knew the secret. I'm simply thankful I've experienced the feeling because I'm sure there are those who never have.

WHEN BILLY PLAYED SECOND BASE, it was scary the way we worked off one another. The way we thought about baseball, the way we learned about baseball, the way we communicated about the game. The fact that we were brothers helped. We had a certain level of communication that far exceeded the level I had with any other human being. Through words, the way each of us moved, we understood each other like no one else.

It was far different playing with Billy than anyone else. We thought the same way, and we wanted to do well together. It's not critical, but to be the very best you can be in terms of execution in the infield, it's an advantage to really know the other person.

Just look at some of the best double play combinations. Alan Trammell and Lou Whitaker have reached a point far beyond normal combinations because they have spent so much time turning the double play, playing side by side, dealing with situations, talking, being out on the field together. They do everything instinctively because they know the runners, they know each other's strengths, they know when they can turn the double play, when they can't. They just know each other.

When Billy was here, I felt I had that situation. I felt like he had played next to me for ten years when it had been only a season. Each year I felt like we became even better.

The more we played together, the more success we experienced. It was so easy.

I remember looking in from shortstop to see what the pitch was going to be, and the batter was swinging back and forth, the bat down low and blocking my vision. It was a critical stage, and there could be a hit-and-run because I saw Tony LaRussa over there and I know he likes to hit-and-run with this batter in this situation. I was trying to get an indication of what the pitch is so I could determine coverage.

If it's a fastball away I know I'm going to cover second base on a double play. If it's a breaking ball or a change-up, then I'm going to give coverage to Billy. So I'm looking, and the hitter keeps waving his bat.

Suddenly, the pitcher's in his windup and there's a moment of panic, and I look over to Billy and say, "I didn't see the signal." And Billy instinctively says, "You." He did not say whether the pitch was a fastball or a change-up, he just gave me coverage because he knew that told me everything.

In that split second I'm able to figure out that the pitch must be a fastball, and everything just quickly falls into place. I don't know if that can be achieved with somebody else, because Billy knew exactly why I needed to know the pitch.

He knew I understood it could have been a hit-and-run situation. He knew what I was trying to find out and why. So instead of telling me the pitch, he skipped two steps. After the play I explained why I didn't see the pitch and that I needed to know. He just said, "I know."

In certain critical situations, when we needed a double play, we didn't have to discuss it or explain anything to each other. Any ground ball was two outs, and I knew what my responsibility was to him, and he knew what his responsibility was to me. We both knew exactly what the other would do.

If it's a slow-hit ball, it's going to be a close play. I had to make up the difference by throwing the ball where he wanted it. Billy used to call it putting the ball in his holster, his right hip outside the bag. I knew if it was one of those fringe double plays I had to put the ball at the back of the bag so he could shift his weight, catch and let it go. I knew if I got the ball right there he would turn the double play. And it was important to know all that.

SOME NIGHTS, even long after games, I'll replay in my mind all the plays I made. I know many of them probably looked like they were a routine. But sometimes there are tricky ones that no one else sees. Sometimes I know I'm really ready for the play. I know exactly where the ball is going to be hit, I anticipate, get there quickly, and throw him out.

From where I started, that should have been a difficult play. I'll look at my spike marks in the dirt and the distance from third base, and it confirms the difficulty. And that makes me feel good. The ultimate compliment is to make a tough play look easy, even if no one else notices.

We were playing at Oakland, and Mike Bordick hit a little dribbler. Football had recently been played on the field, so it wasn't in good condition. I'm coming in, and at the last minute when I'm in front of the ball ready to pull it in and throw it to first, the ball takes a bad hop.

Suddenly I'm out of rhythm. Now I have to adjust and throw, bang, bang. I was able to make the play and get off an accurate throw, but as I was running off the field I'm thinking, ''It almost got me.'' No one else really knew what had just happened.

KNOW AN AUTOGRAPH on a ticket stub or a popcorn box can seal a very special memory. Or catching a foul ball, which is very difficult to do, can be something a boy or girl never forgets. Now they have this ball, and they put it on their dresser—or, if they are like me, sleep with it. I had all those same feelings growing up.

Don Baylor gave me a glove when he was playing for my dad in Triple A. I cherished that glove. And I was very possessive of other things. I kept all the minor league programs and all the inserts with the names of the players. I would cut out the rosters and paste them a certain way.

There's a flavor to baseball and that's unique to each individual. I was never an autograph kind of person, but autographing was always part of baseball. I knew what an autograph meant because I knew what balls and bats and gloves meant to me.

So instead of souring on the whole autograph thing, with adults using kids to collect signatures, I have tried to focus on the positive effect it can have. This year, with the streak and the celebration, I realized the importance of making myself available to sign. I didn't feel any additional responsibility to

repair the damages caused by the strike. I was just caught up in the joy of baseball. I can honestly say I didn't sign one autograph in the hopes of winning back fans. I think that would have been short-sighted. If you're going to sign then sign, because you want to.

When I was a kid, a player might give me a cracked bat. I'd put it in my room, look at it, pick it up, and play with it. At that moment I could remember the circumstances that led to my receiving that bat. I'd put some nails in it, tape it up, and use it. But I still brought the bat back to my room and put it in the corner so I could look at it. I equate signing a ticket stub or a ball to those memories.

When I was looking for houses a few years ago, I was taken through a house that still had people living there. I went into the kid's room and looked around at all the stuff, and up on the dresser there was a ball I had signed. It was sitting right on top of the dresser where I would have had my ball, or shiny rock, or whatever I thought was important at the time.

The fact that it was on top of the dresser, the same place I put my things, struck me.

"It was powerful and magical, an almost out of body experience."

AS THE RECORD-BREAKING GAME came closer, I experienced what must have been a case of nerves. I wasn't worried about going out to play, but it was the thought of something building and not quite knowing what was going to happen, if it was going to happen, how it was going to happen.

It felt similar to the days leading up to my marriage—the anxiety and excitement that come with such a special moment in your life.

I had a fever the last three or four days before breaking the record. I felt sick. I couldn't sleep at night. I would get so hot that I'd sweat through my clothes, the sheets, and the comforter. Then I'd get cold. I thought maybe I had a flu bug, but I realized I didn't have any other symptoms.

I remember feeling run down, but I just figured it was nerves. During the days leading up to the record event, I really didn't sleep. I wasn't having nightmares or anything like that, but I'd suddenly find myself wide awake.

I RECALLED GAMES AND EVENTS from the past, especially during the California series or "streak week," as they called it in Baltimore. I remembered going into the outfield at Memorial Stadium during batting practice when I needed time to myself. I tried, using one of my dad's sayings, to "preserve a state of mind."

Sometimes you can harness anger during the course of a game and turn it into a positive. But generally you have to have a good frame of mind and outlook to be consistent.

I remember I wasn't hitting well in 1988, and I was getting all kinds of flak about playing every day, how I was hurting the team. While I was trying to digest all these thoughts, I was also confused by them.

The criticism was so contrary to my beliefs about baseball and life. Here I was, defending my desire to play. In the end, I came to the ballpark, and the manager either put me in the lineup or he didn't.

I always thought the manager wanted me in there, so it was easy. All I had to do was play. I went out to left-center field and leaned against the fence, trying to figure out what the meaning of the streak was, when Brady Anderson came over. I told him I wanted to be left alone with my thoughts, but he wouldn't leave. So I posed the question: What does the streak mean to you? He thought it was a great thing. I knew it was important to Brady.

I knew the attention I received during 1995 spring training foreshadowed what was going to happen during the course of the season. I knew people were going to recognize me more and maybe see us play more. I didn't necessarily think my popularity would grow, but I knew the awareness of what I was doing every day was going to increase.

And the more people wanted to know about me, the more I opened up. I just tried to go with the flow and handle the situation the best I could. I tried to be as accommodating as possible and deal with everything happening around me the right way.

I wouldn't say there was a price to pay, but there were ramifications from all the attention. Intellectually, I knew my life would change, maybe only subtly, but I had to adjust to those changes.

I feel like I'm in a period of adjustment. I'm trying to keep everything in perspective by thinking of myself only as a baseball player. And that is what I am, a baseball player with certain talents. I love to play, and I'm thankful for the opportunity and all the great things that have happened to me.

But I know that doesn't make me a better person. Even though I've gained a great deal of attention, and many people think the streak is a great thing, I still have to fight to keep it all in perspective. Let's not forget that I'm just a baseball player.

Sometimes I feel a conflict because others are saying, "You've done something that's going to be remembered throughout the history of baseball," and all the other nice words people have spoken. So I'm trying to gain a balance between what I've done and who I am. During the last part of the season, it really became an internal struggle.

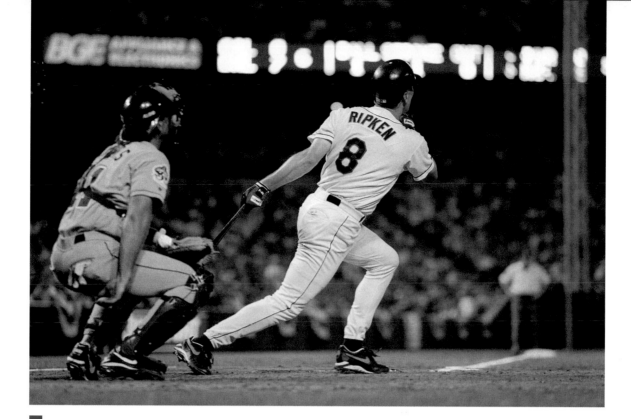

THROUGHOUT MY CAREER, whenever I've really wanted to do well—situations like an All-Star Game—I just couldn't do it. It seemed like the harder I tried and the more I wanted something specific to happen, the less chance I had of making it happen.

In my case, the more relaxed I am, the better I perform. I knew I needed to get myself into a state of mind where my abilities took over as I neared the record. I wanted to do well so badly in the California series because I knew it would enhance the whole celebration. But coming into that series I just wasn't consistent.

Once the series started, I was tinkering with my stance like I always did, and there was a highlight from 1991 on the scoreboard. I had a squat stance where I opened up more than I do now. Mike Mussina was watching the board, and he said, "Remember that stance? Try that."

Jim Abbott was pitching, and it was a day game. I went up there, spread out a little bit, and hit a home run.

The next night—game 2,130—I came up late in the game and felt Herculean because the adrenaline was running so high. No matter how tired I might have been, I remember feeling like I could hit one out of the stadium. It seemed like my focus was there on every pitch. So I popped the ball to left-center field. I really didn't think I hit the ball hard enough to go out, but it ended up going over the fence.

Then, on the record-breaking night, the count went to 3-0 in my second at bat. Historically, I've been a bad 3-0 hitter. But I remember thinking, "If there was ever a time to get a good pitch, this was it." I was telling myself, "Think it's 2-0 or 1-0. Be ready." Right then my concentration locked in, and I was in that zone.

The ball came in slow. I felt like I cocked the bat back slowly, and bam! I watched it go out and took about two steps before everything returned to fast motion and I heard the crowd scream.

WITH EVERYTHING HAPPENING around the streak, I was forced to dig deep inside myself to find out what it all meant to me and who I most wanted to share the experience with. I knew I wanted to share everything with my immediate family—my mother and father, brothers and sister, and my wife and kids. Then the one player I thought of was Eddie Murray, who really guided me and directed me and molded me into the player I am today.

As I analyzed my whole career, I knew I had learned through my dad's teachings and my experiences of being around him and playing the game myself. I had come to understand the idea of not getting too high when you're going good or too low when things aren't going well. I understood that ups and downs were simply part of a game that is played every day. I knew that the right way was to play on a regular basis.

But what's a regular basis? Depending upon the definition, that might mean taking ten or twenty games off every year. Maybe it meant playing five out of seven days or six out of seven days. At the beginning, I really didn't have an idea what playing regularly meant. I had the desire to play, I wanted to be there, and physically I was capable of doing it.

Eddie was there early on to put me on the right track in an environment that was strange to me. Once Eddie befriended me and made me feel comfortable, he showed me the way. He did not say, "Look kid, this is how you play the game." He showed me through his actions, by showing up every day and being in the lineup. Eddie showed me how important it was for a player of his stature to be in the lineup every day, how important it was in the eighth inning of a ball game to be out there at first base.

By witnessing Eddie and talking to him, I developed a deeper understanding of how to play the game. All the teaching I had growing up and my experiences in the minor league came together. I had been listening to and watching others, but Eddie was my prime example.

His desire and his pride are phenomenal. That's why he's the player he is. So I followed his example, and I now know why my career went in the direction it has. My dad told me to be there on a regular basis, and maybe that meant if I'm tired one day and don't feel like playing, then I could take a day off. Without Eddie, I never would have understood the full extent or meaning of being there every day.

I FELT A LITTLE EMBARRASSED by all the attention I was getting, especially when the president and vice president came to the record-breaking game. Then to have them stop in to see me—I felt honored beyond comprehension.

I found myself trying to understand why the president of the United States would be at a baseball game talking to me. I guess that's the part that made me a little self-conscious.

The president talked to me about the importance of the streak and how people were now talking about their perfect attendance at work. He said I provided a good example. That really made me feel good.

While I didn't set out to be a role model, I understand athletes are in a position to influence people. I always thought it was just as easy to watch yourself and try to be positive as it was to ignore the situation.

But the president talked to me just like a guy talking to another guy. I gave him an Oriole's jacket, and I told him, "I want to give you something I never have an opportunity to wear because I've been playing all these games." He kind of laughed at that. I also gave him two commemorative balls and bats and signed them.

There was a comical side to the moment. I was still sweating a lot because I had a fever. So right when I began talking to him I started sweating badly. I was trying to sign the bat for the president, and I had beads of sweat dropping all over it. I was thinking to myself, "I know I sweat a lot, but..."

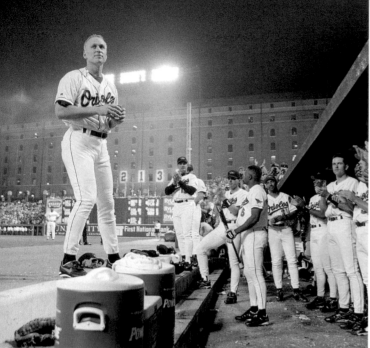

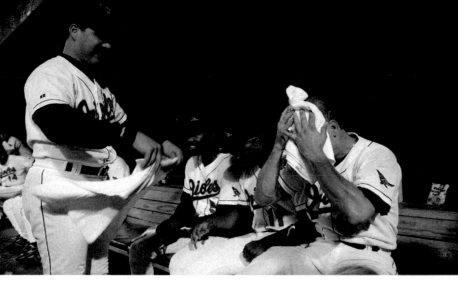

I'M STILL APPRECIATIVE of how the record was received and how people reacted. I tried to express my feelings without words. On that night, I wanted the people of Baltimore to know what they had meant to me. I went through some ups and downs, and they were always there for me.

And it struck me that maybe they didn't know how thankful I was for all the support I've received. I wanted them to know. And I wanted to share the moment with my wife and kids. I knew ahead of time that I wanted to give my jersey and hat to my son and daughter, but I didn't know how or when I would do that. Then I found the right moment.

It was so emotional for me that I needed to be with them. My daughter is at an age where she has a good understanding of things, but she's still young. There was no way she could grasp what was going on. Neither did I, for that matter.

It was so overwhelming for me that I can't imagine how it must have been for my children. I think my daughter liked the noise, the celebration, the clapping. She understood that it was a special day for me because my wife had been talking to her for some time about what was going on.

At our house on September 6, we had talked about how it was a special day for me and Rachel because it also was her first day of school. So when I went over to see them during the game, my daughter kissed me on

my forehead. And I was sweating so much that after she kissed me, she wiped her mouth. I'm sure a lot of people thought she was wiping away the kiss, but it was really the sweat. I remember her saying, "Oh daddy, you're all sweaty."

That morning my daughter had given me the T-shirt I wore under my uniform that night. So I made sure I turned around and showed her that I did what I said I would and wore the shirt. It was one of the most powerful moments I could ever imagine.

I guess I came out of the dugout four times after the record was set, and it seemed like the ovation was getting louder. My teammates, Rafael Palmeiro and Bobby Bonilla, said, "We're never going to get this game finished unless you run around the stadium." I told them I didn't think I had the energy. Finally they picked me up and pushed me out there.

I knew it was the right thing to do as soon as I made eye contact with a fan. Suddenly the relationship with the crowd became more intimate. As I looked into their eyes, the connection became more intense. I started seeing people I knew or recognized.

I'm the kind of player who is normally oblivious as to who's in the park. Then all of a sudden, I started recognizing people who had been coming to games for years. And once I did, I could see a feeling of happiness and celebration.

I never really thought about the Angels in their dugout until I got there and saw everyone standing. Rod Carew said something to me that was very special. It was so strange to be received this way by an opposing team. To shake the hands of the opposing players during a game—any game—just doesn't happen. It was a great moment for baseball.

INTELLECTUALLY, I think I now know what the record means. To me it was a phenomenal event and a very special day—one I'll never experience again. The way it unfolded was powerful and magical, almost an out-of-body experience.

There are certain events in life—for me, my marriage and witnessing the birth of my children—when you feel as if you are able to pull back and view yourself going through the moment. That's how I felt on the record-setting night. I was able to watch myself.